THE PROPHET OF SELF- EDUCATION
Presents

"SAY WORD"

By Daniel A Hopkins
(Mr. Maxx Moses)

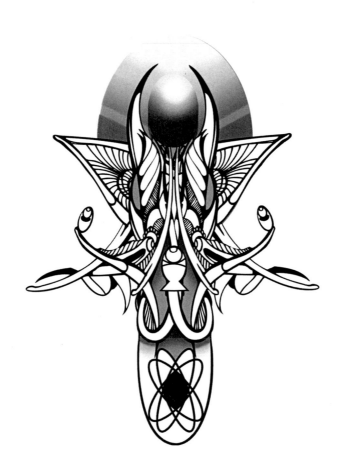

"I LIVE TO CREATE"

To Lance...
CREATIVE For life!

Maxx Moses...

Copyright © 2016
PROPHET OF SELF-EDUCATION BOOKS

Printed in the United States of America
First Printing, July 2016
ISBN 978-0-692-7578-6

Prophet Of Self-Education Books
325 W. Washington Street #2112
San Diego Ca. 92103

Contact (619) 416 4832
www.maxxmoses.com

ART & AFFIRMATION

Affirmations are here as reminders, for we are Forgetful. We've forgotten the beauty from which we've been created. We need constant reminders of our oneness with everything in creation to alleviate the pain of loneliness. Art is here simply to remind us of being Hueman, of being divine. Because placing value only in things we can quantify diminishes the beauty of the energy behind the substance.

Daily, we must internalize and speak words of life into our heart's mind. This type of food nourishes the spirit and calms our being, creating space for peace clarity and love.

Use these affirmations as mantras and the images to help you visualize. Read memorize and recite them while you transform your hearts mind. Eventually you will begin creating your own mantras and images. Write them down, draw them out and guide your destiny with living, breathing words of life.

Awaken

The idea of trust is intertwined with relationships. In order for us to relay love and encourage one another there must be trust. Trust is built over time and once trust is established there is a foundation for stability. Maintaining stability is a practice. Recognizing how our actions affect others is consciousness. Awakened ones work at purifying their thoughts and deeds towards harmony the natural rhythm of life.

At the feet of what example do we sit and honor the ideal of trust? My first brick of trust came from my parents who stayed together and raised our family. My brother and I trusted mom and dad to feed clothe and guide our infancy into adulthood. Outside of our family nucleus it was the community that willingly intervened when they witnessed us acting out of sync with our family's values. For this I am forever grateful.

As we got older, we were taught to trust the institutions of religion, government and corporations. I sensed imbalance and contradiction within their ideals, which clashed with my inner being. My family made sense. My community made sense, the rest of the world began to smell like bullshit. I lost trust in these doctrines of double standards. So I rebelled and wrote my name over everything. It was the realest and most freeing experience of my teenage life. I devoted my life to this practice and while the rest of the world viewed my writings as a crime, I was freeing my mind one tag at a time.

This was my spiritual awaking!

Do The Work

Challenging situations often snatch us out of our comfort zone so fast our only reaction is fear. This fear fast tracks our minds to write horrific endings for unknown situations. We are then surprised when the outcome of the occurrence is unfavorable, as if we played no role in the writing of this script.

A painter simply chooses the colors he wishes for the desired outcome of his painting. He has conditioned his mind towards creating a favorable outcome. He diligently works through all the uncomfortable aspects of the creative process and perseveres, for in his mind beauty and mastery awaits him.

Every hue-man is an Artist. Meditate and quiet your mind and create space, for "love is space." Then gratefully awaken everyday and color your thoughts. Use SAY WORD to help visualize and affirm your inner strength and mental magnetism. Be potent and speak life into your existence, of a life that represents self- love and higher purpose living.

My mind is a factory of joy that cooperates with my Heart and Soul. I make music, I sing, I dance, "I live to create. "

I meditate. It quiets my mind and strengthens
my spirit.

I am uncontrolled by outer circumstances,
Instead I listen to my inner voice
and it guides me.

My positive spiritual energy
is stronger than any negative
thought, feeling or person.

I am responsible for my own happiness.
Therefore, I will cultivate and work hard to maintain it.

The presence of the Divine is at the forefront
of my mind.

I am the courage, the comfort and the strength
that dispels all fear... I breathe deeply.

Relaxed, poised and powerful
I move through my days wanting
only to be in alignment with the
universal flow.

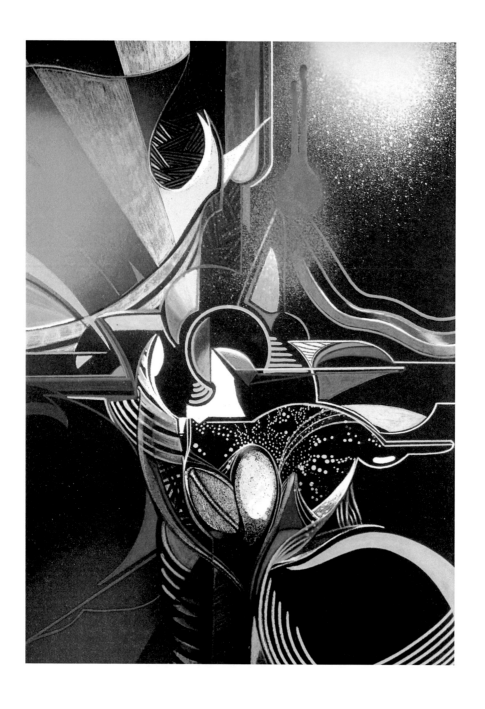

I thrive in uncertainty and the unknown is
my paradise of discovery.

I reflect and recognize that life is all about
relationships. The wonderful people we meet
along the way, all seem to be in our lives at the
right place and time.

May your accomplishments bring you joy
and your state of being become a rock of strength,
throughout all circumstances.

I am the creator of beauty in my thoughts and feelings. I am the creator of beauty within my family, my community and the world at large.

I am a fearless warrior that walks the planet creating,
living, giving and receiving.

I pay attention to my breath, the shallow and the deep, feeling the presence of the divine within every inhale and exhale.

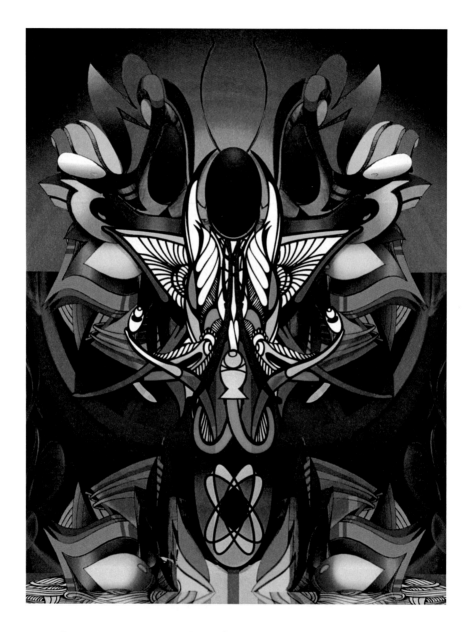

There are no mistakes just experiences.
The only mistake is the idea of a mistake.

I will pay attention to my energy.
I will pay attention to my energy.
I will pay attention to my energy.

I am worthy of my greatness
I am worthy of my ordinariness I am worthy
of all my desires and the peace that resides within.

Be comfortable with being uncomfortable.
Pay attention to this uneasiness and uncover what's
hiding beneath your emotions.

Everywhere I am, there is magic all around me.
I am aware of who I am. I am grateful
for this moment.

I carefully select my words and articulate my ideas.
for they are powerful instruments of
manifestation.

My being is being still, whole and complete.

When our need to be RIGHT has overridden the
need to be in harmony, we are out of balance.

Never be afraid of who you have to become. Next.

There is only one thing to do in life.
And, that is your life's purpose.

I am eternal. I am eternal. I am eternal.

I recognize, that the challenges of life are designed to
push me beyond myself constructed boundaries.
Ultimately propelling me, to deeper and richer levels of
love and understanding.

Believing is for a child's mind. Knowing is reality.
And when the heart and the mind are unified its
Divine knowing.

My imagination fuels my creativity. My creativity ignites
my spirit. And my spirit finds joy when it emerges
from the cocoon of darkness. I flap my wings,
it's a new life, again.

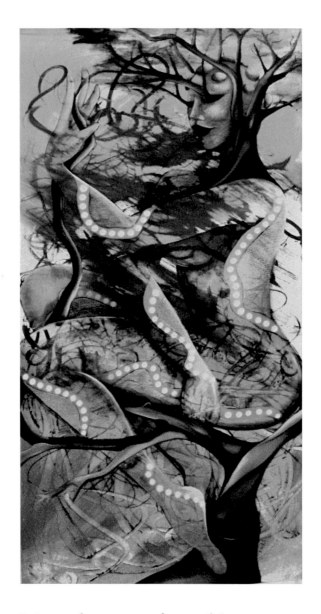

My values are found in nature.
How I treat the earth and everything
around me is a reflection of who I am.

I am the rhythm of Chaos and Order.
I ride the waves through the seasons of change.
Meanwhile, cultivating my Inner garden for the
harvest of harmony and prosperity.

I must be honest with myself.
In order to grow, I must release myself
from my conditioned mind and awaken to
the truth and the light of reality.

The light, in my mind my body and my spirit
shines forth with the potency of our Ancestors.
They seeded this Earth with knowledge, wisdom
and understanding.

I look toward my Ancestors for guidance.
Their wisdom prepares me to fight the
injustice, that shadows our world with darkness.

Together we are unified in a bond
that knows no separateness. I am
Yoga, we are one.

I live a purpose driven life. And my name is my identity.
Reminding me of who I AM and why I AM here.

"Love is Space" and although I may not agree with you, I honor your place on this earth, to live life as you see it.

Pose 2, is a teacher and a visionary. Thus the name POSE stands for the Prophet Of Self Education. His Art, which is seeded in self- discovery and transformation, is his practice. Emblazoning his name upon New York City subways is where he began. The SUNY College at Brockport is where he initiated the fusion of what the world calls Graffiti with Fine Art.

Upon graduation and returning home to Yonkers New York, Pose 2 founded Unscene Wildstyles, an art manufacturing company that employed 11 high school students. The company's success and impact upon the community was so insightful that the Yonkers City Council cited him with a Proclamation award. However, his return home was short lived.

Always in search of inspiration, Pose moved to Philadelphia, Pennsylvania raised his family and Founded the BBOY BBQ. This annual gathering of Spray Can Artist, Break Dancers D-Jays and more has grown into a Festival, which is now celebrated in Rochester New York and Copenhagen Denmark. While in Pennsylvania, he had the opportunity to collaborate with the Philadelphia Mural Arts Program: painting murals, working within prisons, writing curriculums and leading workshops. Equipped with a portfolio of skills, he moved on.

He journeyed to California, changed his name to Maxx Moses and ignited his intuitive creative process, Concrete Alchemy: the transformation of blank walls into objects of beauty and community energy. This new vision, with its vast horizon of openness affected his color palette mentally and physically. He brought the BBOY BBQ to California and wrote his first play for dance theater, "Graffiti Life…The Color of My Sole."

Maxx Moses sees the world as his community, inspired through painting murals, conducting workshops and sharing insights. Abu Dhabi, Dubai, Lebanon, Italy, Peru and Zimbabwe are a few destinations he's had the opportunity to enrich and be enriched. These experiences have taught him the value of relationships and how much we interdepend upon one another to live, grow and thrive.

"Only The Strong Survive"

This book is dedicated to my nucleus family. My Father, Frederick Hopkins, 88 years young is the cornerstone of our family and still remains as the living legacy of consistency, grace and dignity. Pops, I love you and thank you for simply being you.

My Mother, Marion Hopkins, who transitioned in May of 2005, was the fire in my life. It was her creative spirit and unpredictability that captured my attention. Her resourcefulness astounded me, her fearlessness was natural, her will and determination relentless. And, at the end of each day she'd play her favorite record over and over again… "Only The Strong Survive." She instilled in us the qualities of life that empowered us to stand up and be the men we are supposed to be. For this, I am forever grateful Moms may your spirit find serenity and peace for eternity.

My Brother, Ronald Hopkins, whom I adore is the grandest big brother any kid brother could ever have. He is a natural leader, a lover, a teacher and the purest example of manhood I know. The conversations about life and its deeper meanings began with him. We've always shared our books, stories and dreams. Between us, there was this hunger to answer some of life's basic questions. Who are we, and why are we here? I thank you big brother for always being available.

These are my first teachers, the Hopkins Family.

52423280R00028

Made in the USA
San Bernardino, CA
19 August 2017